Green Hill

Green Hill

POEMS BY
Lorna Knowles Blake

WINNER OF THE 2017 ABLE MUSE BOOK AWARD

ABLE MUSE PRESS

Printed in the United States of America

Library of Congress Control Number: 2018931557

ISBN 978-1-77349-010-6 (paperback)
ISBN 978-1-77349-011-3 (digital)

Cover image: "Starry Passage" by Alexander Pepple
(with "fenced greens" by Levi Bare)

Cover & book design by Alexander Pepple

Able Muse Press is an imprint of *Able Muse:* A Review of Poetry, Prose & Art—at
www.ablemuse.com

Able Muse Press
467 Saratoga Avenue #602
San Jose, CA 95129

for all the Blake Girls

Acknowledgments

I am grateful to the editors of the following journals where many of these poems originally appeared, sometimes in slightly different forms:

American Arts Quarterly: "A Nest"

Brilliant Corners: "Duke Ellington"

The Cortland Review: "Fable" and "Misdemeanors"

Duct: from "Proverbs of Hell": "Bring out number, weight, and measure in a year of dearth," "The cut worm forgives the plow," and "The crow wished everything was black, the owl that everything was white"

Heliotrope: "Nabokov's Blues"

The Hudson Review: "Glosa," "Sketches of Lorca," "Testimony of the Senses," and *"Urna votiva"*

Literary Imagination: "Ino's Veil" and "Ode to Books"

Mass Poetry: "Sisters"

Mezzo Cammin: "The Allure of the Ledge" and "On a Line from 'Astrophel and Stella'"

Big City Lit: "Caracole," "The Garden as She Left It," and "Manna"

Radius: "Mackerel Sky"

Raintown Review: "Passacaglia"

The Same: "Aliens," "Celestial Navigation," "The Happy Composer," "Baucis and Philemon," and *"Retorno"*

The Tampa Review: "Persephone in Manhattan"

Verse Wisconsin: "Lullaby"

"Duke Ellington" also appeared in *The Cento: A Collection of Collage Poems,* edited by Theresa Malphrus Welford (Red Hen Press, 2011).

"Prepositional" appeared in the anthology, *The Waiting Room Reader, Volume II: Words to Keep You Company,* by Roxanne Hoffman and Richard Mark Weinraub, edited by Rachel Hadas (Cavankerry Press, 2013).

"Sketches of Lorca" also appeared in *Verde que te quiero verde: Poems after Garcia Lorca,* edited by Natalie Peeterse (Open Country Press, 2016).

The full translation of Rubén Darío's sonnet *"Urna votiva"* also appeared in the anthology *Poets Translate Poets,* edited by Paula Dietz (Syracuse University Press, 2014).

The poem "Green Hill" is dedicated to Waveney "Kip" McGough Blake and to Barbara "Sparks" Elliott Hopkins. May their memories be for a blessing.

Deepest thanks to Able Muse Press: contest judge Charles Martin and publisher Alex Pepple for making this book possible; to Annie Finch for her invaluable editorial advice; to Peter Campion, Mark Doty, Jehanne Dubrow, Anya Groner, Rachel Hadas, Alice Kociemba, Molly Peacock, and Vijay Seshadri for their encouragement; to my dear friends and trusted readers for their time and attention; to my beloved dogs for their creaturely comfort and to my family—especially and always to my husband and daughter—for their endless love and constant support.

Contents

Green Hill

I

Big hoarfrost stars come with a fish of shadow . . .

Intertidal

Twice a day, the pageantry
repeats: high tide eddies out,
leaving hard-packed sand,

the bay's debris,

twined in marsh grass. Under
driftwood, treasure abounds.
So, too, the forgotten plastic

shovel, broken

bottle, flip-flop sandal from
Brazil. How far it has traveled
in tendrils of seaweed, motion

of moon, water

delivering bones, stones, shells
of snails and crabs and clams,
some cracked, some translucent,

intact, waiting

for the next inhabitant: whelk,
periwinkle, hermit crab. I, too,
feel like an eremite. One cold

morning, I fail

to find anything I've lost in the
wrack, despite my silent search.
Give me *strike that.* Fetch up

a sign—any sign.

A Nest

In autumn we found a wren's empty nest,
nested in the berry canes, a tangled braid,
braid of grass, bark and twigs, made for rest,
rest and nurture, sheltered in deep shade
that shelters nothing now, "A reminder,
memento mori," you said, and made a space
(*another* space!) among our books and clutter;
our cluttered shelf the tiny home's new place,
re-placed from spring's earthy, vegetal shade,
it casts a shade-filled reverie of rest—
small forests rustle through this slender braid,
braided feathers, wool, and catkins: a nest.

Lullaby

In the lamp's arc, in your little bed-boat
you are ferried to sleep by pictures and words;
a ritual ballast to keep you afloat—
in the lamp's glow, your bed rocks like a boat
on a deep sea and the story's a moat
against monsters, against all night hazards.
See? The lamp is a moon, your bed is a boat
and sleep is a river of pictures and words . . .

Ode to Books

I think of you as the smallest forest,
             leaf after leaf
          of paper smelling like a sheaf
of wheat, of elemental things, things blessed,

and as the open door, the swinging gate
             to all we know
          and don't know, sunlight and shadow,
a lamp-lit room, the hour growing late . . .

The human castle rises stone by stone—
             sorrow mortared
          with beauty waits between the hard
and soft covers of these books we try to own.

after Neruda

Fable

Dawn: a vixen at the verge
of lawn—she's red-blur,

dream-thought; now vanished
to an earth-nest in the woods

behind the shed; apparitional
again at dusk. Fooler of Crows.

Night: scream of cottontails;
her sharp, cough-like barks.

Now come the blonde kits
to spoil our vines. They strip

berry canes, leave droppings
in neat, purple piles and roll

on new sod carpets. Sunlight,
grass, the dogs indoors, asleep,

no dangling grapes to sour
the day: nothing out of reach.

Proverbs of Hell

William Blake

VI. The cut worm forgives the plow

O Plow, thou art quick.
The invisible worm
That lies in your path
In the furrowed ground

Has forgiven your blade
Of hardened steel,
The horse that pulled you,
And the cart's cold wheel.

Sketches of Lorca

I have lost myself in the sea many times.
—"Gacela of the Flight"

It's winter and the night is cold, but still he feels
the fever of the sea; thirsty water seeking new forms,
sprawling across land, overflowing the silver pools
and stone cisterns. Purple roses and white camellias
hang, waiting to fall from a trellis of violet shadows.
Love stirs in the blood: love, a tumult in the heart,
fierce as fire blazing in snow, salt rubbed in a wound
that never heals. Sheltered by plaster and jasmine,
asleep on a bench in the silent courtyard, he dreams
he's losing himself—he's lost again—in the sea.

Mimosa

Far beyond the casement-framed perspective,
a riot of pink inflorescence swirled
    Mimosa
    Hermosa
on the pane promises a rose-colored world,
but transparency can be deceptive.

Walking up from the beach at noon we see
only a brushstroke of blush on a green
    Mimosa
    Hermosa
foreground of locust and aspen trees that screen
the house from view and, behind us, the sea . . .

Now, as the window admits half-gray skies,
the tree, in her pink-petal prom girl dress
    Mimosa
    Hermosa
that charmed the garden, is a spindled mess—
every year she blooms, every year she dies.

Twombly's Tulips

The parrot tulip caught
his eye, his painter's heart,
and his imagination.

Gripped by *tulpenwoede,*
his own tulip mania
was a craze of sap green,
orange, magenta; taught
by masters of his art—
pictorial combination.

These blooms are sepia:
essence of tulip, not
color reduced to part
but tulips, deeply seen,
and blurred to abstraction.

Baucis and Philemon

. . . Beneath the map of age their savoured youth.
— Dick Davis

Years ago, when it was warm, they loved and fought and loved;
like animals at night they moved: they never dreamed of harm,

and recklessly they did and said whatever their hot blood chose
and afterward their hot blood rose and swept them off to bed.

Later the bed was calm and still when children came to rest,
one child asleep, one at the breast, and yet love had its fill . . .

The children grew, the sun shone high, time made its strict demands:
the children grew and made their plans. Stars wheeled across the sky,

and plans were scrapped or rearranged. The life they'd first begun,
under a slow, benignant sun, began to turn and change.

More briskly now, the sea winds blow; their small boat sails across
an ocean of loss and still more loss, and who can claim to know

what love has been, what love will be, here in the north, the cold,
where they are both now growing old—

                              will he go first? will she?

15

Prepositional

Above our heads, a ceiling.

Across the ceiling, a wide sky.

Around the house, birdsong.

Between you and me, a table.

On the table, bread and salt.

Behind us, breadcrumbs

Against a wandering forest.

Before this, a long wandering.

Beneath us, a rich meadow.

Or beneath us, quicksand.

Since then meadows, quicksand.

In you, something, as of a raft.

In me, something like weather.

Beyond us, the unfailing tides . . .

II

Green, how I want you green,
Green wind, green branches.

Love Your Rhythm

"Ama tu ritmo"

Love your rhythm and place your actions
under its laws, as well as your verses;
you are a universe of universes
and your soul is a fount of creation.

You presuppose that a celestial union
will cause the varied worlds in you to burst
forth, and as your numbers, echoing, disperse
you'll pythagorize your constellations.

Listen to the rhetoric in the divine
notes of the airborne bird, discern
night's colors, geometrically combined.

Kill that indifference so taciturn
and string pearl after pearl, crystalline
where truth overtumbles her urn.

translated from the Spanish of Rubén Darío

Retorno

Like tiny green dragons, lizards flick
their tongues, tree frogs chirp,

as I take photographs in failing
sunlight. I live elsewhere now, in a land

with no street, no tree, no scent
of childhood. Where is home?

I ask my dead grandmother,
who is sitting on her plaid suitcase

by the curb. It's right here,
she tells me. There—see?

Your house, your room, your bed
with its carved headboard and you

dreaming in it—here, on the shifting
coastline of memory.

Glosa

The fish taken out of the sea
Is not without a consolation:
Its dying is of brief duration
And ultimately brings relief.
 — Saint John of the Cross

Far from myself, in pain and yet
not feeling, I'm sunk into a trance.
All around me, the cosmic dance
goes on, its beautiful motet,
its counterpoint and pirouette . . .
Is this how I am loved? So well
that I am prisoner in a hell
devised of tears and sleep? Beset
by nothing I can name, I envy
the fish taken out of the sea—

a shock like that has sweet appeal.
The force of elemental change
might cause the brain to rearrange
and set the body free to feel
the hook, the dock, the sun, the real
experience of its own end,
and the soul (for let us pretend
there is a soul, and it can heal),
in that moment of sensation,
is not without a consolation,

flown from its chamber of disease.
My soul rejects both love and food;
all I can do is tend my mood
and stare into its vortices,
ignoring those insistent pleas—
We need milk, Love, you have to call
the plumber. Mom? There is a wall
to scale, and I am on my knees.
Is a fish more than a person?
Its dying is of brief duration,

so different from yours: how long
your dying took, Mother, compared
with what we'd hoped; how unprepared
we were, and you, afraid and strong
at once, in that slow evensong
of loud machines and spongy shoes.
My sorrow gone, I'd stand to lose
you twice. The counselors are wrong:
it's more a state than stages, grief,
and living there brings me relief.

Duke Ellington

once said, "The memory of things gone is important

In a Sentimental Mood, Mood Indigo,

to a jazz musician." Jazz is the memory of things—

Perdido, Flamingo, Lotus Blossom, Solitude,

things gone. The memory of the musician is important;

Prelude to a Kiss, Sophisticated Lady, Satin Doll,

the jazz musician is gone and so many things are gone.

I Got It Bad and That Ain't Good, All Too Soon,

jazz is important to the memory of things gone.

Moon Mist, Day Dream, Drawing Room Blues,

What is gone? The music of things, the memories . . .

Blue Serge, Lover Man, Caravan, Chelsea Bridge,

The memory of things gone is important to a jazz musician.

Jump for Joy, Come Sunday, Take the "A" Train.

Proverbs of Hell

William Blake

XIV. Bring out number, weight, and measure in a year of dearth

The year after he died, she cooked, and not
as if the two of them were at the table, but

as if the whole family were expected for supper:
all her numbered dead. She weighed the meat,

then measured out ingredients for a banquet
every day. The foods they loved and the foods

they hated that were good for them, recipes
passed down from other countries, other times.

In this way, she transformed a year of dearth
into a year of plenty and threw it out each night.

The Lepidopterist

To love with all one's soul and leave the rest to fate.
— Vladimir Nabokov

Protected here, his
angel wings, morphos,
fritillaries float,

suspended like fine
jewels in a vitrine.
Chromatic display

of colors now pinned
in shadow boxes
cannot blur the air

with their sudden small
brushstrokes or quicken
the pulse of summer.

Neotropical Blues:
Pseudolucia,
Lysandra cormion,

each suffused with shrill
disquieting details:
flashing eye spots, scales

that seem to tremble
on lanceolate wings
spread, ready to fly,

powered by sunlight,
into the perils
of their migration.

Mackerel Sky

in memory of Rachel Wetzsteon

The day I learned you died, the Crescent City's
sky was blank and bright. I ached, not to stop
all the clocks, but to fill the sky for you—
no single inch of blue, a vault of silver scales.

I am now the foster mother of your book
of clouds. A book we both had thought to buy,
seduced by the review (halos, sun dogs,
coronas!). When I saw it on your shelf

it pained me: unlike you, I hadn't bought
the Book of Clouds, though I, too, love them,
faithful shapeshifters. Now, it's in my mind
we talk of clouds: no Upper West Side park

bench conversations, no Cape Cod bayside
ooohs and aaahs over sun pillars, nimbus
inflamed by the sunset, no Rorschach games:
you see cannonball sacks; I counter, sheep.

Your cloud poems are open on my lap
today; I glance at *water in the cirrus
drifting east* and think, *sometimes a cigar . . .*
This evening, clouds bank, crepuscular.

Sketches of Lorca

Nobody eats oranges under the full moon.
One must eat fruit that is green and cold.
— "The Moon Rising"

Oh, how the world adores his fiery name,
his cold, cold moons, the weddings of blood,
the mournful passions that pace and slouch
beneath iron Andalusian nights full of songs
and castanets: flamenco in the plaza, caped men
singing of love racing through veins; desire spreading
like ivy over alabaster flesh; the beloved dreaming
of kisses under the stars, while the *sereno* calls
the hours from midnight to dawn, and jilted lovers
sit, defiantly peeling oranges under a full moon.

Passacaglia

8:48 a.m.

Some say ghostly trains are seen gliding into
graveyards, stopping at midnight. No one ever
hears the whistle. Passengers shuffle aboard,
        carrying nothing.

8:50 a.m.

Kneeling buses, hum of construction, traffic.
Bass harmonic: rumble and clack of morning—
city, borne on a steady chord progression
        moving in triple time.

8:55 a.m.

Street noise: wailing sirens and strident klaxons
puncture droning memories. Landscapes, faces
flash by. I've been traveling miles. Subway station,
        swelling with music.

Caracole

Tiny enamel spiral,
designed with exquisite art,
recently abandoned—
a snail's shell in the grass
catches the light at daybreak.
Overturned, exposed, vacant,
its coiled intimacy
has the ransacked air
of a refugee's home
the day after the raid.
Naked, vulnerable
to a thousand inclemencies,
the exile seeks shelter,
if only by building itself
another small stone prison.

Green Hill

So many ways to remember a house:
a blue sketch on a white card, an address. . . .
But why, when I arrive, is the lot empty?
A village, yet the loved house stands alone.
In photographs, it is facing the harbor,
that place of return, and of no return.
A hermit crab, I carry my house everywhere:
no house I choose will be my home forever.
Four walls, but it's the contents of the crates,
they say, make a home, which a house is not.
At night, an adagio of appliances, and breath,
house composed of ocean, birdsong, moonlight.
Verde que te quiero verde. Green I love you green
wind-house, leaning on the edge of a hill.

Not four walls, just the contents of the crates:
houses built of ocean, birdsong, moonlight.
A hermit crab, I carry my house everywhere.
They said make a home, which a shell is not.
Verde que te quiero verde, green I want you green.
At night, adagios of appliances, and breath,
but which house will be my home forever?
Wind-house, leaning into the long, green hill.
In the village, my loved house stood alone.
And then I arrived, but the rooms were empty.
A blue sketch on a white card, an address
in my sleep, always facing the harbor.
It is a place of return and of no return—
This is one way to dream about a house.

III

Let me climb up! Let me, up to the green balconies.

El teleférico

Caracas, Venezuela

She was falling into the opening sky:
into strawberry farms, snow-capped
trees, *la Sierra Nevada;* it's how it was,
that year or two when she was four.

A bomb exploded in the street
and there were pink ballet lessons.
They took a trip up to the mountain
peak, past the roof of the world,

on the cable car. See the snow
forest? Hold on, don't be afraid.
Look, look! Tiny towns falling all
away, then the cable car swayed—

The Allure of the Ledge

His left hand bolted to the narrow frame,
      his feet in dancer's second on a ledge,
      precariously balanced at the edge
of atmosphere and masonry—no game,

      but he's been tempting fate behind a scrim
of screen and soot, insouciant as he draws
his sponge across the pane without a pause.
      This crisp blue fear is oxygen to him,

he's hanging there, inhaling razored air,
      hitching his leather strap to rusty hooks,
      rocking in ever higher cradles. Books
never appealed except to serve as stairs

      to windowsills, which even as a child he'd climb
and balance on, leaning outward calling,
"Watch me fly!" then quickly falling inward.
      Up here, he turns dark rectangles of grime

into skies of dripping clouds, while below
      toy cars and buses navigate the town,
      and swaying in his harness he looks down
to orient himself because he knows

      it's looking *up* that causes vertigo.

Aliens

No One Can Hear You Scream in Space—
or see the terrified look in your eyes,
your hunted, haunted, ashen face.
No one can hear a scream in space
although it echoes in every place,
in the dreadful emptiness of eyes
of everyone we've loved who dies.
What is grief but a scream in space?

Proverbs of Hell

William Blake

*LXIII. The crow wished everything was black, the owl that
everything was white*

A crow's invisible at night—
black wing, black eye *(caw caw)*
the owl, nocturnal, hunts by sight.
A crow, invisible at night
because he isn't snowy white,
eludes the owl's beak and claw.
A crow's invisible at night—
black wing, black eye *(caw caw)*.

If every living thing were white,
an owl would clearly see *(who who);*
a moon can make a light more bright
and every living thing more white. . . .
A clear down-drop, the bloody swoop—
much easier to hunt by night
if every living thing were white:
the owl could see his prey *(who who)*.

Celestial Navigation

And all I ask is a tall ship and a star to steer her by . . .
— John Masefield

We've jettisoned the sextant and the art
of reading skies: a folded map, the chart
of constellations old sailors knew by heart—
these all now play a sad, superfluous part

in every voyage. Satellites above
are closing in: they calculate, my love,
our destination; their mathematics move
us onward ever faster as they prove

technology can guide us anywhere.
Goodbye, Dog Star, Major and Minor Bear.
Farewell, Orion. Pleaïdes, are you there?
Will you be, as increasingly we stare

ahead (not up) for signals from afar?
A global system tells us where we are:
we're found or lost . . . but wait! There *is* a star
—Polaris—in the dashboard of our car.

Habits of Deception

Fibs

Those false
affidavits
submitted in defense
of diligence—the dog, the mail,
the train . . .

A Mortal Lie

Love aimed
her question mark,
and Heart, too quick, fired back.
Their duel made a casualty
of Trust.

Lying in Bed

Ceded
to separate selves
on each side of the bed
they whisper—Did you . . . Yes. *Of course!*
Did *you*?

The False Witness

I swear
by all that I
believe in—only I
believe in nothing—hence can swear
to all.

White Lies

Such quaint
dissemblers, clad
in snowy dimity
but homespun, brown and sturdy, shows
beneath.

"Vissi d'arte"

Just as she'd have Cavaradossi change
his painted Magdalen's eyes to smoldering brown
from limpid blue, I've mentally revised
a scene or two. This Sunday matinee
let orders not be given, let torture not
ensue, let lovers, secured by safe conduct,
make their escape on the old village road—
and Scarpia!—no merciful knife for him.

Face it: no one's here for happy endings.
Like citizens of Athens we're improved
by tragedy: the hero's sacrifice,
the dastard's end, the diva's harrowed pain.
O deadly promises! O cruel forgotten fan!

Act III: You clear your throat and squeeze my hand.

Ino's Veil

Homer, *Odyssey, Book V*

Rising from her salty underwater cave, she spread
her scarf, recalling all the times it had been a tree

whose branches collected her, nested and singing,
how, under her slim white ankles it had become

a stairway, cloud, or pillow on the water; a scroll
for verses written with a feather dipped in the sea;

while at other times the veil was glassy as a mirror,
or gossamer as a spider's web, always transforming

what it reflected or caught. She tossed it in the air
and twirled it, draped it over her shoulders lightly

and then, with a snap of her wrist, she cast her veil
upon the waves to save Odysseus from the sea god.

Sisters

Eagle Head, Manchester, Massachusetts (High Tide) [1870].
— Winslow Homer

The eldest, who anticipates the tide,
is standing, hair capped, slightly to one side
and at right angles to both other girls.

The middle one, face hidden from our view,
is shaking out her wet and yellow hair,
and as she does, she sprays the other two,

while the youngest, hunched upon the sand,
looks up in frank annoyance as the cold
saltwater stings her face and each drop lands:

a surrogate for worn insults and spats.
Their small red-collared puppy seems about
to jump back with a yappy bark, and that's

a matter of contention, too: which he loves best.
Love is contention always, as they test
its boundaries. Whose flag was planted first?

The self in each they know to be unique
is sometimes contradicted when they speak
in the same voice, or when a gesture's shared,

or when a feature (ankle, neck, or knee)
is slightly changed by reproduction's whim.
A different night, and *she* might be *you* or *me,*

as Homer saw, that North Shore afternoon,
blending their shadows on the sand in places.
One girl looks up—mirror of two other faces.

from *Urna votiva*

My work, if I could work the stone,
releasing the marble's cold fire,
I'd crown with a rose and a lyre.

My dream, as day turns back night?
To see in the face of a weeping girl
one tear full of love and of light. . . .

translated from the Spanish of Rubén Darío

Misdemeanors

Thievery *is* exciting.
Audacity, too, we envy,
and Daring, and Wagers.
Furthermore (with its
implied "tsk, tsk"), Risk
of any kind: snooping,
filching coins, sneaking
booze and cigarettes,
illicit affairs, rubber
checks, stacked decks,
bald-faced lies, fingers
crossed behind our back,
light-fingered:
                    Pocket
the thing. Palm it. Look
over your shoulder.
                    Run.

Persephone in Manhattan

Checks that mother is asleep
              on a sofa garden of chintz,
book still open, tea cold—

sneaks out of the apartment,
              streaks past doorman, dog
                           walker, corner panhandler.

              Rushing to dim the glare
       of her green, sunlit potential,
she crosses against the light

to a forbidden entrance
       leading down to places
              night-blooming, fluorescent.

              Danger holds the door for her,
       sweet escort to that nether city
of dark corners: smoke-filled

bars, clubs where she, greedy,
       samples the shiny garnet seeds,
              seeds of the world's pulpy fruit.

       How can she now return to you,
to your yellow fields and flowers,
       to your blooming, tangled love?

IV

But who will come? And where from?

Sketches of Lorca

Few are the angels that sing.
— "Cásida of the Lament"

The muezzin's call falls silent, the *converso's* prayer
seeps into the sand and tears muzzle the wind.
Then history returns with its swords and decrees—
above the gray walls of Granada, the sky opens
every window in every house onto a balcony
veiled in latticed sunlight. He leans over the railing,
holding a thousand violins in the palm of his hand,
and hears the *cante jondo* of gypsies thread the air.
Even the dogs are quiet in the night and the violins
tune their strings to the angels' immense lament.

Testimony of the Senses

On earth you never must rely
on what the senses understand.
— Saint John of the Cross

Lowing cows, cello
notes, mobbing birds (*seet,*
seet, chick-a-dee-dee),
claxon, choir, surf-roar,
silence, breath, breathing. . . .

Blood on the tongue; taste
of sex in the mouth,
salty. Wine, lemons,
and sweetness: dripping
berries, plums, ripe figs.

Flesh rotting (rodent,
clipped by the mower),
scent of linden trees,
midsummer rain, stale
tobacco, warm bread.

Skinned pelt, infant skin,
soft bruise, red welt; hands
grip, slap; lips on nape
of neck, kiss—*yes*—feel
love's caress; love's bite.

Sky, scraped by shadow;
maple, blazing; stained
glass; starlight; phosphor;
pixels; pitch dark; ice
storm; sudden sunlight.

Overture

In a dark house, at the conductor's touch,
a baton waves a single note of music
into a vibrant symphony. So many hands—

hands playing, one touch and then the music.

Frost Lines: A Cento

Oh, let's go up the hill and scare ourselves,

War is for everyone, for children, too.
A sea, about the towns where war has come. . . .

That still, if I repent, I may recall it—
A field that stretches toward the North,

Seeing myself well lost once more, I sighed.
Where had all my weariness gone, and why

Had the prophet of disaster ceased to shout?

One such storm in a lifetime couldn't teach us,
But stars were scarce in that part of the sky.

Argos

Vigil over, Argos, exhausted, flattens
his ears, lowers his tail and dies. Today,
watching the dog wait at the door for hours,
       I can believe it.

Patient-hearted hunter, neglected, flea-bitten.
Where is your Odysseus? Aged beyond knowing,
striding home, the warrior spies his loyal hound
       rising to greet him.

Where is his Odysseus? Errand or war,
it's the same to him, dumb, devoted creature.
Good dog. I say, *He'll be back.* I promise you.
       Ithaca's waiting.

The Happy Composer

I would not want to go under without having written something—no more than a page—that goes to the heart.
— Ernest Chausson (1855–1899) to Claude Debussy

Born to wealth, supported by
his father's fortune, he was free to roam
the countryside and picnic in the grass;
indulge in evenings warmed by claret and cigars,
under rows of silver-framed daguerreotypes
on mantelpieces, while at the shawl-draped
piano, his lovely wife, her plump hands pink
beneath the kerosene lamp's smoky glow,
played every piece he wrote, darned his socks
and packed his lunch that summer day, the sun
high and bright, the air vibrant with birdsong,
the baguette still warm in its wrapper. And then
the rock, that fateful rock in the path, a rock
that caught the rim of his bicycle wheel—
and that absurd fling over the handlebars
and the terrible fall that killed him, instantly.

The Garden as She Left It

The dim figure of the woman,
The recent flutter of hands.
> — Sarah Hannah (1966–2007)

query
Oh, why did you leave the garden, friend? Tell
us. Didn't we cultivate the flowers you adore,
their common names so unlike common ground—
milk thistle, pencil flower, mother-of-thyme?

reply
Blessed thistle, sky pencil, creeping thyme. . . .
Double names, double selves. One day I found
a wild flower in a cold, furious bed and tore
it out. I was gone. There's nothing left to tell.

On a Line from "Astrophil and Stella"

This garden irritates—a spate of crude,
late blossoms lingering past October frost:
one sullen rose; a ragged little brood
of lilies by the pond; and by the post,
a blowsy dahlia with an attitude
of cool defiance is vamping on and on,
inelegant and passionate. It isn't rude,
she still insists, to overstay the season.

O treacherous middle years! My mood,
despite this Indian summer, is autumnal
and even in my greenhouse chills intrude
from time to time. I've tried the usual
remedies—music, art, and solitude—
But, "Ah," Desire still cries, "give me some food."

Manna

Even in this grim, immutable
month there are signs—
forbearance in the stripped trees,
patience in the packed ground.

Each day, the wind chides,
each day, enough will be given.

Sketches of Lorca

America drowns itself in machines and lament.
— "Ode to Walt Whitman"

He came searching for angels in the dark eclipses
of New York; under immense, curved stairways,
up and down chaotic, angry streets, in parks strewn
with abandoned objects wrapped in barbed wire
and death. Nothing flowered from the bitter root
of progress, only apples tasting of gasoline,
doves rising in chains to agitate the sky, and fear
disguised in dirty needles of rain. Where, he cried,
is the old poet, with his beard full of butterflies
and the boys, the beautiful boys, singing by the river?

Proverbs of Hell

William Blake

VII. Dip him in the river who loves water

Dip him
      in the water of the river
Dip him
      in the river
            of the water
In the river,
      in the water,
            in the river
      in the river
            in the water
Rivers love the water
        love the water
Water loves the river
        loves the river
Dip him
      in the water, in the water
In the river,
      dip who loves the water
Dip him
      in the river
        who loves water.

Ararat

No longer afraid, the animals grew restless,
      our sons argued in the night, their wives, sick,
querulous, refused to leave the hold.
      He stayed above, laughing in the storm,

            Husband, I see you—

hair wild in the wind, the dove alert on his shoulder.
      Drunk all day in the vineyard after the flood,
missing the deck's roll, the spin of wheel against palm,
      the ark's yaw and pitch.

             lying there naked, shaming your sons—

      truth is—*Husband, I know you*—he needed
the wine, needed sea legs to walk on this hard land.

pp. 3, 17, 33, 49: The sections' epigraphs are from Lorca's *"Romance sonámbulo,"* translated by William Bryant Logan as "Sleepwalking Ballad," in the anthology *Rose, Where Did You Get That Red? Teaching Great Poetry to Children* by Kenneth Koch (Vintage Books, 1990).

pp. 12, 28, 51, 61: The "Sketches of Lorca" poems contain phrases and images from the poems by Federico García Lorca attributed in the epigraphs, from my own translations.

p. 13: "Mimosa" is indebted to James Merrill's "Pola Diva" for the form.

pp. 21, 52: The epigraphs are respectively from "I Live Yet Do Not Live in Me" and "For All the Beauty There May Be," by St. John of the Cross, from *The Poems of St. John of the Cross,* translated by Willis Barnstone (New Directions, 1972).

p. 23: "Duke Ellington" is a cento composed from a quote in the *New York Times* editorial celebrating the centenary of his birth on April 29, 1999. The song titles in italics are taken from the compact disc *Duke Ellington's Greatest Hits* (RCA Victor, 1996).

p. 31: "Green Hill" is inspired by Rachel Hadas's "Body of a Book."

p. 37: "Aliens" is taken from the tagline "In space, no one can hear you scream," from the movie *Alien* (1979), directed by Ridley Scott.

p. 55: "Frost Lines: A Cento" lines come from the following poems by Robert Frost: "The Bonfire," "The Broken Drought," "Lost in Heaven," and "Our Singing Strength."

p. 58: "The Garden as She Left It" title is taken from Sarah Hannah's memoir-in-verse, *Inflorescence* (Tupelo Press, 2006). Many of the flower names come from her poems.

p. 59: "On a Line from 'Astrophil and Stella'" references the last line of "Astrophel and Stella LXXI: Who will in fairest book of Nature know" by Sir Philip Sidney.

LORNA KNOWLES BLAKE lives in New Orleans and Cape Cod. Her first poetry collection, *Permanent Address,* won the Richard Snyder Award and was published by Ashland University Press in 2008. She serves on the editorial board of the journal *Barrow Street* and on the advisory board of *Poetry Sunday*, a weekly program of WCAI, Cape Cod's public radio station. Her poems, translations, essays, and reviews appear regularly in literary journals, both in print and online.

ALSO FROM ABLE MUSE PRESS

Richard Newman, *All the Wasted Beauty of the World – Poems*

Alfred Nicol, *Animal Psalms – Poems*

Frank Osen, *Virtue, Big as Sin (Able Muse Book Award for Poetry)*

Alexander Pepple (Editor), *Able Muse Anthology;*
Able Muse – a review of poetry, prose & art
(semiannual, winter 2010 on)

James Pollock, *Sailing to Babylon – Poems*

Aaron Poochigian, *The Cosmic Purr – Poems;*
Manhattanite (Able Muse Book Award for Poetry)

Jennifer Reeser, *Indigenous – Poems*

John Ridland, *Sir Gawain and the Green Knight (Anonymous) – Translation*
Pearl (Anonymous) – Translation

Stephen Scaer, *Pumpkin Chucking – Poems*

Hollis Seamon, *Corporeality – Stories*

Ed Shacklee, *The Blind Loon: A Bestiary*

Carrie Shipers, *Cause for Concern (Able Muse Book Award for Poetry)*

Matthew Buckley Smith, *Dirge for an Imaginary World*
(Able Muse Book Award for Poetry)

Barbara Ellen Sorensen, *Compositions of the Dead Playing Flutes – Poems*

Rosemerry Wahtola Trommer, *Naked for Tea – Poems*

Wendy Videlock, *Slingshots and Love Plums – Poems;*
The Dark Gnu and Other Poems;
Nevertheless – Poems

Richard Wakefield, *A Vertical Mile – Poems*

Gail White, *Asperity Street – Poems*

Chelsea Woodard, *Vellum – Poems*

www.ablemusepress.com